CONTENTS

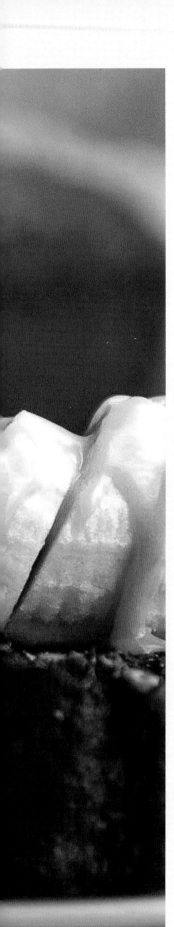

INTRODUCTION

Cooking should be fun!

As a mother of two lovely children and a lover of good food, I realized that in order to build a healthy relationship with food, every meal should be memorable, unique, creative and at the same time, fun! Meal prep should not tire you out so much that you can't enjoy your meal neither should it be boring or unexciting.

That's why I created this recipe book!

In my many years of cooking, experimenting and making it fun, I have gathered amazing tips and recipes to create a wide range of delicious food.

In this book, I have taken wonderful flavours that make up your classic meals and have presented them to you in a way that makes it easy and fun for you to prepare. Whether you're having a large family over, or you're cosy-ing up with your pet cat, you're sure to have fun and flavour with these recipes. They are easy-to-follow and the ingredients, easy to find. You will find recipes ranging from pastries to snacks, sauces, chicken dishes, and even smoothies.

I'll encourage you to take on the challenge to try your hand at all the 25 recipes in this book. Who knows if a master chef resides in you? (*wink emoji*)

I can't wait for you and yours to enjoy the most delicious, yummy, tasty, flavourful, scrumptious, delightful meals!

Let's get to it!

Love,
Belle

EQUIPMENT LIST

ESSENTIAL UTENSILS

Measuring cups/spoons

Whisk (non-stick)

Potato masher

Vegetable peeler

Box grater

Small knife

Spatula

Kitchen scissors

Garlic crusher

Wooden spoons

Non-stick pot/pan

Baking pan/tin

ESSENTIAL MISCELLANEOUS EQUIPMENT

Chopping board

Measuring jugs

Kitchen timer

Sieve

Mixing bowls

Baking parchment

Food storage containers

Cooling rack

Spraying oil

ESSENTIAL ELECTRICAL EQUIPMENT

Scales

Electric hand mixer or stand mixer

Food processor or mini chopper

STORE CUPBOARD LIST

Baking and Sweet List

Cocoa Powder

Flour

Baking powder and Bicarbonate of Soda

Maple syrup

Brown sugar/white sugar

Ground cinnamon

Milk chocolate bars

Vanilla extract

Lemon extract

BASIC COOKING INGREDIENT LIST

Suya spice

Pepper soup spice

Njansa seeds

Black pepper

Scotch bonnets

Olive oil

Coconut oil

Ground/fresh ginger

Garlic

Ground cumin

Himalayan salt

Onions

Paprika pepper

Tomatoes

Palm oil

Corn flour

Bay leaves

Cameroon pepper

Nutmeg

Bouillon powder (Maggi brand)

Liquid aminos

Maggi liquid seasoning

NAUTTY BANANA CAKE

INGREDIENTS

1 tablespoon baking powder

1 teaspoon baking soda

2 medium bananas

1 ⅓ cups of plain flour

1 cup dark brown sugar

1/3 cup coconut flakes

1 teaspoon vanilla paste

1 teaspoon lemon extract

1/3 cup pecans

125g butter (melted)

3 eggs at room temperature

METHOD

1. Preheat oven to 160° C and prepare baking tin by lining with a parchment paper. Then, set aside.

2. Peel bananas, place in a bowl and mash together until pureed. Then, add the melted butter followed by sugar and coconut flakes.

3. Sift in the flour, baking powder and baking soda.

4. Add the eggs and whisk to combine using a whisk.

5. Once combined, add the pecans and pour into a lined baking pan (leave out some pecans for topping).

6. Add toppings and place in preheated oven, bake for 50 minutes or until it is risen and golden brown.

7. Allow to cool before slicing.

FREEZING AND DEFROSTING TIP

Banana bread freezes well. To properly freeze it, cut in slices and wrap with cling film. Then place in a freezer bag and freeze. To defrost, heat in microwave for 30 seconds.

CARAMEL GLAZED CINNAMON ROLL

INGREDIENTS

Dough

3 cups of bread flour or all-purpose flour (483g)

1/2 cup whole milk

1 tablespoon fast action dried yeast

2 eggs at room temperature

65g unsalted butter at room temperature (cut into small cubes)

3 tablespoons white sugar

3 tablespoons water

Pinch of salt

Filling

1 cup of dark brown sugar

1 tablespoon cinnamon powder

65g milk chocolate

50g of butter (melted)

METHOD

1. Place milk in a microwavable jug, warm for 45 seconds.

2. Add yeast to the warm milk and stir with fork to combine; set aside for 8 minutes.

3. In a stand mixer bowl; sift in the flour, add sugar, and salt. 8 minutes later, add in yeast. Rinse in the jug with 3 tablespoons water and add in the stand mixer bowl. Using a dough hook, combine at speed 1 for 5 minutes.

4. Now increase speed to 3 and continue the kneading process. Add the eggs and continue to knead for 3 minutes.

5. Once combined, add the butter; knead for 4 minutes until dough looks smooth and silky.

6. Transfer dough on a slightly floured work surface, bring dough together to form a sphere/large ball.

7. Lightly grease a bowl, place the dough, cover with cling film and a towel; leave in warm area for 1- 2 hours.

8. Punch off the air, then place on a floured work surface and roll out into a rectangular shape (42cm by 32cm rectangle)

9. Using a pastry brush, coat the rolled dough with melted butter. Mix the sugar and cinnamon together. Then cover butter brushed dough with cinnamon-sugar mix and sprinkle the chocolate.

10. With the longest edge closest to you, roll the dough up into a cylinder. Cut into 10 even slices, using a thread or a knife.

11. Place in a greased baking tin, cover with towel and place in a warm place for 45 minutes for second proofing.

12. Place in a preheated oven; gas 180°C and bake for 20 minutes until golden brown.

13. Allow to cool down; glaze with homemade salted caramel toffee glazing, serve warm.

BANANA CARAMEL SWIRL CAKE

INGREDIENTS

1 cup dark cocoa powder (102g)

1 cup plain flour (133g)

3 medium bananas (494g)

3 eggs (200g)

170g butter, melted

½ cup sugar

1 teaspoon baking powder

1 and ½ teaspoon baking soda

¼ cup coconut flakes

¼ cup chopped hazelnuts

3 tablespoons caramel sauce

1 teaspoon vanilla extract

½ teaspoon lemon extract

Milk chocolate bars

METHOD

1. Preheat oven at 160°C and line baking tin.

2. In a bowl, place peeled bananas in a bowl and mash until pureed.

3. Add the butter, sugar, vanilla, lemon and coconut flakes. Now, sift in the cocoa, plain flour, baking soda and baking powder.

4. Using a whisk, combine all together. Once combined, add the hazelnuts, and stir in.

5. Transfer into the lined baking tin, scoop in the caramel sauce. Using a skewer, swirl it. Then, top with broken milk chocolate pieces and bake in the oven at 170°C for 45 minutes.

6. Allow to cool before slicing.

SALTED CARAMEL SAUCE

INGREDIENTS

1 cup double cream

4 tablespoons dark brown sugar

1 teaspoon salt

100g toffee fudge

3 x (1/3 cup) icing sugar

METHOD

1. In a microwavable jug or bowl, add double cream, salt and sugar.

2. Microwave for 4 minutes; occasionally stir every 1 minute.

3. Once out of the microwave; add the toffee fudges and stir using a whisk, until completely melted.

4. Place icing sugar in a small cup, add 3 tablespoons of the caramel microwaved sauce, and mix until dissolved and smooth in texture.

5. Transfer all back into the caramel sauce bowl and stir until combined.

6. Allow to completely cool before using. Store in an airtight container and place in the fridge

MORNING FAT FLUSH

INGREDIENTS

1 whole pineapple (850g)

1 bunch organic celery (580g)

94g ginger

METHOD

1. Peel the pineapple and cut into 6 equal parts.

2. Wash the celery.

3. Peel skin off ginger.

4. Then juice. Drink straight away or pour in an air tight flask/container and store in the fridge.

This juice is better drunk on an empty stomach.

ENERGY BOOST SMOOTHIE

INGREDIENTS

METHOD

1 medium avocado (161g)

1 cup of almond or soya milk

2 tablespoons honey or maple syrup

1. Scoop out the avocado from its casing and place in a blender.

2. Add the milk and syrup to the blender also and blend until smooth.

3. Share in glasses and enjoy

BROCCOLI BEEF SUYA SAUCE

INGREDIENTS

300g broccoli (cut into bite sizes)

150g king prawns (washed)

3 spring onions (sliced)

3 shallots (sliced)

200g beef suya

3 tablespoons melted butter

2 garlic gloves(minced)

salt or seasoning powder to taste

Gravy Mix

1⅓ cups of beef stock/broth

1 tablespoon low sodium soy sauce

1 tablespoon liquid aminos

1/2 teaspoon ground black pepper

2 tablespoons corn starch

3 tablespoons maple syrup

METHOD

1. In a non-stick pot, over a medium to high heat, add butter and heat up. Once heated, add shallots and ginger; fry until fragranced.

2. Then add the broccoli, season with salt or seasoning powder and fry for 5 minutes.

3. Add the prawns and beef suya and continue frying for the next minute.

4. In a small bowl, add all the gravy mix ingredients; stir and add into the pot. Stir and allow to simmer further on medium heat until sauce thickens.

5. Turn off heat and serve hot with rice.

CARAMEL COCONUT CANDY

INGREDIENTS

2 whole coconuts

2 cups sugar

½ teaspoon salt

3 X (1/3 cups of coconut flakes)

¼ cup caramel sauce (refer to page 10 for the caramel sauce recipe)

METHOD

1. Crack the coconuts and remove from casing. Wash properly and grate.

2. Place a non-stick pan over high heat, add the sugar and allow to melt; stir occasionally to avoid overheating.

3. After 5 minutes or once completely dissolved and golden brown in colour, add the caramel sauce and stir. Once you notice it's bubbling, turn off heat.

4. Now add the grated coconuts and coconut flakes, transfer pot to the lowest burner and reduce heat to the lowest.

5. Stir fry until coconuts are well coated. Continue to fry for 3 – 5 minutes. Now turn off heat and allow to completely cool.

6. Using a cling film, wrap into small balls individually and place in the fridge. Allow to further cool down before eating

SHORTCRUST PASTRY 1

INGREDIENTS

600g plain flour

300g salted butter (straight from the fridge)

200ml tap water

METHOD

1. Sift the flour into a mixing bowl. Cut the butter into smaller pieces and add in the bowl.

2. Using your fingertips, rub the ingredients together until the mixture looks like breadcrumbs. As you're doing this, lift your finger above the bowl as you rub them to incorporate some air.

3. Add milk and combine until the dough comes together, leaving the bowl clean.

4. Wrap with cling film and put in the fridge to chill for 30 minutes before rolling.

SHORTCRUST PASTRY 2

INGREDIENTS

245ml whole milk

500g flour

250g salted butter

MERRY HAND PIES

INGREDIENTS

1 shortcrust pastry 1 (refer to page 16)

2 large potatoes (505g)

3 large carrots (388g)

1 medium spring onion

1 onion (176g)

1kg beef mince

1 tablespoon oil

1 teaspoon salt

1½ teaspoons bouillon powder

1 teaspoon ginger

1 teaspoon white pepper

1 teaspoon corn flour

150ml water

Ingredients for Egg wash

1 egg

2 teaspoons milk

METHOD

1. Pre-heat oven at 160°C. Prepare the baking trays by lining with a parchment paper

2. Make up the pastry following recipe for 'Shortcrust Pastry 1' on page 16 Wrap and chill in fridge for 30 minutes.

3. Prepare egg wash by cracking egg into a bowl, add milk, whisk and set aside.

4. Prepare vegetables by cutting/chopping into small cubes. Place a pot over medium heat, add oil and heat up.

5. Add ginger, spring onion and fry until fragranced. Then add the carrots and potatoes, season with ½ teaspoon of salt. Stir fry for 3 minutes. Add the minced beef, bouillon powder, white pepper and remaining salt; stir to combine and continue to stir fry for 8 minutes. Stir occasionally to avoid burning.

6. Add water, stir in and bring to boil. Check taste, adjust accordingly; either by adding extra salt or seasoning.

7. Once it starts boiling, transfer to a lower heat, add the corn starch, stir in and allow to simmer for 30 minutes or until the sauce thickens.

8. Once sauce is ready, allow to cool before use.

9. Bring out the dough from the fridge, place on a lightly floured work surface. Divide dough into smaller portions. Using a rolling pin, take a portion and roll out; not too thin and not too thick.

10. Using a circle cookie cutter, cut out as much circles as you can. Roll out each circle just a little more. Scoop in the filling (do not overfill) in the middle, apply egg wash on the edges and then fold in.

11. Press down the edges using a fork. Transfer to a lined baking tray. Repeat process for the rest of the dough.

12. Once all are placed on a lined baking tray, using a kitchen pastry brush, apply egg wash on the pies, place in the oven at 160°C and bake for 30 – 40 minutes or until golden and shining.

Cooking tip: Continuous stirring of the sauce encourages thickening, as the potatoes act as thickener as well. Do not make the pies when the filling is still hot, otherwise it would melt through the pastry.

Freezer tip: The pies can be frozen before baking and baked individually when needed. Also, already baked pies could be frozen and cooked from frozen for 10 minutes in oven at 160°C.

SMOKED CHICKEN STOCK

INGREDIENTS

1000g smoked chicken

1000g goat meat

1 tablespoon Himalayan salt

2 tablespoons bouillon powder

1 tablespoon Cameroon pepper

1 large onion

3 bay leaves

500ml water

METHOD

1. Wash thoroughly goat meat and smoked chicken; place in a pressure pot pan.

2. Add the rest of the ingredients and water, cover pressure pot and cook for 14 minutes.

3. Allow cooling, before opening the pressure pot.

4. Separate meat and stock. Further separate the smoked chicken and goat meat.

5. Fry goat meat and freeze for future use and set the smoked chicken aside for cooking native smoked chicken Jollof rice.

SMOKED CHICKEN NATIVE JOLLOF RICE

INGREDIENTS

625g paprika

132g onion

200ml water

1 tomato

1/2 cup palm oil

1 onion

1/4 cup ground crayfish

1200ml stock

2½ cups rice

160g smoked catfish

To Garnish; 1 spring onion and slices of paprika

METHOD

1. Place all ingredients for cooking meat in pressure pot, stir and cook for 14 minutes. Release pressure and allow to completely cool before opening. Remove the meat and save the stock for later.

2. Fry goat meat and set aside. Debone smoked chicken and set aside. Wash smoked catfish in hot water and set aside. Wash rice with warm water until water runs clear and set aside.

3. In a blender, add the paprika peppers, scotch bonnet, ½ onion, tomato and 200ml water. Blend until smooth and pour in a pot; bring to a boil. Allow boiling until it becomes paste.

4. Place a large pot over high heat, heat up palm oil. Add onion and ground crayfish, fry for 3 minutes or until fragranced. Add the paprika paste, and fry. Occasionally stir to avoid burning. Allow frying for 5 – 8 minutes.

5. Add catfish; stir and allow frying for 3 minutes. Now, add smoked chicken stock, stir and bring to boil.

6. Add washed rice, stir and adjust taste by adding extra salt if need be. Add the de-boned smoked chicken, do not stir.

7. Now, cover pot with lid and bring to boil. Once starts boiling, remove lid, cover with foil and place back the lid. Then, transfer to the smallest gas burning, reduce heat to the lowest and allow to steam cook for 40 – 50 minutes or until cooked.

8. Stir rice once cooked, turn off heat. Remove foil and lid, add chopped basil leaves, stir in and place back the foil and lid. Allow to rest for 10 minutes before serving. Garnish with slices paprika and spring onions.

BUTTERFLY SUYA CHICKEN

INGREDIENTS

1 whole chicken (corn-fed chicken)

1/4 cup olive oil

1 teaspoon salt.

1/4 cup Maggi Liquid Seasoning

4 tablespoons suya spice

METHOD

1. Using a kitchen knife or scissors, cut off the chicken backbone. Turn the chicken's front side toward you and cut the collarbone in half. Turn the chicken breast-side up, and press in between breasts firmly with your hand to flatten the chicken. When you hear the cracking sound, you're done.

2. Place chicken in a bowl or freezer bag, add all the ingredients except for the suya spice. Using a thong, mix to coat with ingredients. Cover with cling film or leave in a freezer bag and marinate in the fridge overnight.

3. Heat up grill (electric/oven/outdoor grill). Remove from fridge, add the suya spice, coat on the chicken, leave to rest for 10 minutes.

4. Once grill is heated; place the breast side on the grill and grill for 10 minutes. Then, turn to the other side and grill for 10 minutes (electric grill was used for this part).

5. Preheat oven grill at medium heat (150°C), place chicken in a baking tray breast side up and grill for another 25 minutes or until completely cooked as desired.

6. Serve hot, garnish with onions, cucumber and sprinkle extra suya spice on.

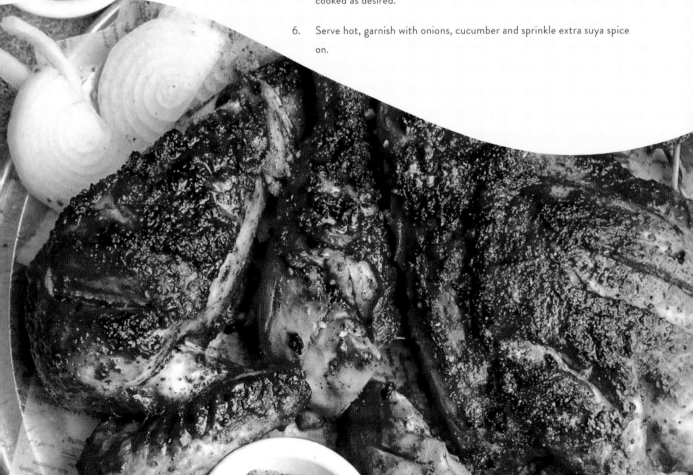

CHICKEN THIGH SUYA SKEWERS

INGREDIENTS

1.2 kg skinless chicken thighs

2 tablespoons Maggi Liquid Seasoning

1/2 teaspoon salt

1/4 cup olive oil

3 tablespoons suya spice

3 mixed bell peppers

1 red onions

METHOD

Preparing the Skewers

Soak skewers in cold water for 30 minutes

1. Cut chicken thighs into thinner slices. Chop onion and bell pepper into big chunks. Place in a bowl, add liquid seasoning, olive oil, salt and combine. Place in the fridge to marinate for 45minutes.

2. Thread the chicken thighs through the skewers, alternating with onion and bell pepper chunks. Now, coat the threaded meat and veggies with the suya spice.

3. Whilst threading through, preheat electric grill. Place on the grill, grill until cooked through as desired.

4. Serve hot. Could be paired with Tortilla wraps.

DELIGHTFUL GIZDODO

INGREDIENTS

Ingredients for Cooking Gizzard

1 kg turkey gizzards

1 tablespoon salt

1 tablespoon bouillon powder

1 tablespoon ground ginger

½ teaspoon dried rosemary

1 onion (sliced)

300 ml water

Ingredients for Gizdodo

1.5kg ripe plantain

1kg paprika peppers

100 ml water

5 tablespoons coconut oil

1 medium red onion

½ teaspoon salt

4 spring onions

½ teaspoon bouillon powder

Oil for deep frying

METHOD

1. Wash gizzards thoroughly and place in a pressure pot pan. Season with 1 tablespoon salt, 1 tablespoon bouillon powder, ginger, rosemary and thyme. Add water and stir. Place in pressure pot, select meat function and cook for 12 minutes.

2. Once cooked, allow cooling before opening the pressure pot. Remove cooked gizzard and slice into tiny pieces; set aside.

3. Heat up oil for deep frying. Peel the plantains, cut into smaller cubes, season with ½ teaspoon salt and fry until golden brown; set aside. Using the same oil, fry the gizzards and set aside.

4. Blend paprika with water, pour blended mix in a pot and boil down until water evaporates.

5. Add coconut oil in a medium pot and heat up. Add in sliced spring onion and onion and fry for 3 minutes. Then add the paprika past. Fry for 8 minutes, stir occasionally to avoid burning. Season with ½ teaspoon bouillon powder and stir to combine. Turn down the heat to the lowest

6. Now, add fried gizzards and allow frying for 2 minutes. Add fried plantain and mix all together. Allow to simmer on low heat for another 3 minutes.

7. Garnish with more spring onions and serve hot.

BANANA LEAF MOI-MOI

INGREDIENTS

2 cups beans

250g paprika

100g onion

20g ginger

25g garlic

1 scotch bonnet

450ml water

2 tablespoons bouillon powder

1 teaspoon salt

½ cup coconut oil

6 boiled eggs (halved)

METHOD

1. Peel beans and soak in warm water overnight. 10 minutes before starting to cook, wash banana leaves and set aside.

2. Prepare some of the ingredients; core the paprika pepper, peel garlic, onion and ginger, wash and set aside.

3. In a blender, add all ingredients except for coconut oil. Once blended, transfer mix into a stand mixer bowl. Hook the whisk and whisk moi-moi batter for 8 minutes on low speed.

4. Remove whisk hook, add coconut oil. Using spatula, mix in until well incorporated into the mix.

5. Fold banana leaves into cone shape (you can watch YouTube to see how) and pour ½ cup moi-moi batter, add egg and wrap.

6. Line a large pot with banana leaves and place all the wrapped moi-moi batter. Cook for 40 minutes on medium to low heat. Serve hot

LEMON FLAVOURED CHIN CHIN

INGREDIENTS

1220g plain flour (8 cups)

176g Nido Powder Milk (1½ cup)

135g sugar (1/2 cup)

2 eggs

160g butter

½ teaspoon freshly ground nutmeg

½ teaspoon vanilla extract

1 teaspoon lemon extract

450 ml water

METHOD

1. Measure all ingredients out. In a large bowl, add flour, nutmeg, powder milk, sugar and butter. Using fingertips or food processor, combine to form crumble-looking mixture.

2. Add eggs, and the extracts. Using hands, combine. Now, add water and combine, once mix comes together, knead to form a smoother dough. Leave to rest for about 10 minutes.

3. Transfer to a lightly floured work surface, divide into smaller parts, for easy rolling.

4. Roll out the dough as thin as possible and cut into desired shape.

5. Heat up oil for deep frying and fry until golden.

NIGERIAN BUNS

INGREDIENTS

3 cups plain flour (523g)

523g plain four (3 cups)

105g powder milk (1 cup)

1/3 cup sugar

1 egg (lightly whisked)

300ml water

50g salted butter

1 teaspoon cinnamon powder

1 teaspoon baking powder

½ teaspoon baking soda

½ teaspoon vanilla extract

½ teaspoon lemon extract

METHOD

1. In a medium bowl; add flour, milk, baking powder, baking soda, sugar and butter. Using fingertips, mix until the mixture looks like a crumble.

2. Stir in; eggs, vanilla, lemon and water; mix well until everything is fully incorporated. The batter should look thick.

3. In a large, medium pot/wok pour frying oil, until it is at least 3 inches of the pot (too little will result in flatter balls), and place on medium to high heat until oil becomes hot.

4. Using hands or spoon, scoop up the batter. If using spoon, use 2 spoons - one to scoop up the batter, and another to drop batter in the oil. Do this in batches, to avoid overcrowding the pot.

5. Fry until both sides are golden brown and cooked through. Repeat process for the rest of the batter. For subsequent batter, turn off the heat when scooping in batter, leave to fry for few minutes before turning them back on.

6. Serve warm and if desired, drizzle some syrup on or roll on icing sugar.

TRIANGLE LAMB PIES

INGREDIENTS

1 X Shortcrust Pastry 2 (refer to page 16)

2 large potatoes (505g)

3 large carrots (388g)

1 medium spring onion

1 onion (176g)

1 kg lamb mince

1 tablespoon oil

1 teaspoon salt

1½ teaspoons bouillon powder

1 teaspoon ginger

1 teaspoon white pepper

1 teaspoon corn flour

150ml water

METHOD

1. Prepare egg wash by cracking eggs into a bowl and whisking. Set aside

2. Pre-heat oven at 160°C. Prepare the baking trays by lining with parchment paper Make up the pastry following recipe on page 16 Wrap and chill in fridge for 30 minutes.

3. Prepare vegetables by cutting/chopping into small cubes. Place a pot over medium heat, add oil and heat up.

4. Add ginger, spring onion and fry until fragranced. Then add the carrots and potatoes, season with ½ teaspoon of salt. Stir fry for 3 minutes. Add the minced lamb, bouillon powder, white pepper and remaining salt; stir to combine and continue to stir fry for 8 minutes. Stir occasionally to avoid burning.

5. Add water, stir in and bring to boil. Check taste, adjust accordingly; either by adding extra salt or seasoning.

6. Once it starts boiling, transfer to a lower heat, add the corn starch, stir in and allow to simmer for 30 minutes or until the sauce thickens.

7. Once sauce is ready, allow to cool before use.

8. Bring out the dough from the fridge, place on a lightly floured work surface. Divide dough into smaller portions, using a rolling pin, take a portion and roll out; not too thin and not too thick.

9. Using a circle cookie cutter, cut out as much circles as you can. Roll out each circle just a little more. Scoop in the filling (do not overfill) in the middle, apply egg wash on the edges and then fold in. Press down the edges using a fork. Transfer to a lined baking tray. Repeat process for the rest of the dough.

10. Once all placed on a lined baking tray, using a kitchen pastry brush, apply egg wash on the pies, place in the oven at 160°C and bake for 30 – 40 minutes or until golden and shining.

CHICKEN PEPPER SOUP

INGREDIENTS

1.4kg broiler chicken (cut into smaller pieces)

2 stalks spring onion

1 large scotch bonnet

92g shallots (3 shallots)

72g cherry tomato

8g ginger

5 garlic (20g)

1 teaspoon olive oil

2 teaspoons chicken bouillon powder

1 tablespoon pepper soup spice

6 njansa

1 tablespoon Himalayan salt

200ml to blend

200ml water for cooking.

Handful Utazi leaves (sliced)

METHOD

1. Soak chicken in water and add salt. Wash thoroughly and place on a sieve. Sprinkle 1 tablespoon of Himalayan salt, toss the chicken and leave on the sieve for about 20 minutes.

2. Transfer salted chicken into a freezer bag and leave in the fridge overnight.

3. In a blender, place ½ scotch bonnet, 2 of 3 shallots, cherry tomato, ginger, garlic, njansa and pepper soup spice. Then add water, blend until smooth. Set aside.

4. Finely slice spring onions, ½ scotch bonnet and the remaining shallots; set aside.

5. Over a high heat, place a medium pot and add oil; heat up. Once heated, add the sliced vegetables and fry for 1 minute.

6. Add the marinated chicken and fry. Fry for 5 minutes; occasionally stir to avoid burning. Now add the blended mix, stir in and cover with lid. Reduce heat to the lowest and allow to simmer for another 5 minutes.

7. Add water, stir in, taste and adjust taste if need be. Cover pot with lid, transfer pot to the lowest burner, reduce heat to the lowest and allow to slow cook for 2 hours, or until meat is tender, as desired.

8. Add the Utazi leaves, stir in and turn off heat. Serve hot

CRISPY CHICKEN BURGER

INGREDIENTS

600g of chicken thighs (skinless and deboned)

300 ml water

1½ tablespoons salt

3 tablespoon apple cider vinegar

3 cups of plain flour

¼ cup corn flour

2 tablespoons suya spice

1 tablespoon smoked paprika

1 Knorr chicken seasoning (crushed)

1 teaspoon ground white pepper

1 teaspoon ground ginger

300ml water

METHOD

1. Place the chicken thighs on a work surface, use a hammer to flatten the chicken. place flattened chicken in the bowl, add water, salt and vinegar.

2. Cover with cling film and leave in the fridge for two hours.

3. In a bowl, add plain flour, corn flour, suya spice, crushed chicken seasoning, white pepper, and paprika.

4. Using a whisk, mix together and set aside.

5. In a large bowl, add water and set aside

6. Using a thong, remove the chicken from the liquid mixture. Place in the flour mix and coat the chicken using the hand.

7. Dust off excess flour, dip chicken completely in water and place back in the flour mix and coat again.

8. Once coated, set aside. Repeat process for remaining chicken.

9. Heat up oil for deep frying. Once heated, place coated chicken thighs in and fry until crispy and golden brown.

EVERYDAY GARLIC 'N CHILL OIL

INGREDIENTS

534g garlic

20g dried Kashmiri chilli

100g shallots

2 cups olive oil

1/4 teaspoon salt

1/4 teaspoon cumin

1/4 teaspoon stock powder

METHOD

1. Preheat grill at 160°C.

2. Share the garlic into 2, place in a microwavable bowl, place each batch in the microwave and microwave for 50 seconds.

3. Repeat same for the second batch. Peel off the casing and set aside.

4. Slice up the shallots and set aside.

5. In an oven proof frying pan, heat up 2 cup olive oil over a medium heat, add garlic, shallots and dried chilli and fry for 3 minutes; stir occasionally.

6. Transfer frying pan into the oven and allow to grill 45 minutes.

7. Allow to cool and transfer into food processor. Process until roughly chopped. Store in a jar.

GOOD MORNING FLUFFY PANCAKE

INGREDIENTS

1½ cup plain flour

1 teaspoon baking powder

1/4 teaspoon baking soda

50g butter (melted)

300ml buttermilk

1 ½ tablespoons whole milk

1 tablespoon fresh lemon juice

1 teaspoon vanilla

3 tablespoons sugar

4 eggs (yolks and whites separated; only 2 yolks are needed for this recipe)

METHOD

1. In a bowl, sift flour, baking powder and baking soda; set aside.

2. Place the egg whites in a stand mixer bowl, add sugar and whisk until forms a white foamy texture.

3. In the dry ingredients bowl, add buttermilk, butter, milk, 2 egg yolks, lemon juice, vanilla and start mixing until a thick and smooth batter is achieved.

4. Over a medium heat, place a non-stick pan and grease; either by brushing with melted butter or cooking spray.

5. Using an ice cream scoop, scoop 3 separate batter into the pan, cook until the underside is golden and the flip over. Cook for about 60 seconds or until the flipped side is golden as well.

6. Transfer to a plate, keep warm by covering with a kitchen towel. Cook remaining batter in batches until all cooked.

7. Serve warm with maple syrup

PROTEIN BLUEBERRY SMOOTHIE

SERVES 2 PEOPLE

INGREDIENTS

180g protein yogurt

150g fresh blueberries

1 cup soya milk

METHOD

1. Wash blueberries thoroughly.

2. Place all ingredients in a blender, blend until smooth. Consume immediately.

ABOUT THE AUTHOR

"Belle Nnorom, an accomplished recipe and content creator, food photographer and brand influencer passionate about good food and healthy living."

I am a "Mummy" to two beautiful kids. My love and passion for cooking started at a very young age, watching my mother cater for schools, meetings and families. By the time I turned 15, she made the easy decision of leaving the catering to me while she carried on with other commitments. I was in love with cooking, creating new recipes, and I would always experiment with flavours to make my dishes stand out. Ma was so proud.

Now, I am a business owner running the company, FOODACE, born out of my passion for memorable dining. I also own a spice range, FOODACE Spices, which is a product of my relentless experimentations to find flavour blends that would go one better than seasonings available on the store shelves.

I am constantly excited to discover and share amazing cooking tips and recipes.

Printed in Great Britain
by Amazon